Lake Powell

GRAND CANYON
NATIONAL PARK,
ARIZONA

GRAND CANYON STATISTICS

Length: 277 miles (measured along the river)

Average width: 10 miles

Average depth: 1 mile

Maximum width: 18 miles

Area of Grand Canyon National Park:

1,904 square miles

NAVAJO
NATION
RESERVATION

Point Imperial

North Rim
Visitor Center

Phantom
Ranch

Cape Royal

HAVASUPAI
INDIAN
RESERVATION

Hermits Rest

Grand Canyon
Visitor Center

Desert View
Visitor Center

For Maeve

Copyright © 2017 Jason Chin

A Neal Porter Book

Published by Roaring Brook Press

Roaring Brook Press is a division of Holtzbrinck Publishing Holdings Limited Partnership

175 Fifth Avenue, New York, New York 10010

The artwork for this book was created with pen and ink, watercolor, and gouache.

mackids.com

Library of Congress Cataloging-in-Publication Data

Names: Chin, Jason, 1978– author.

Title: Grand Canyon / Jason Chin.

Description: First edition. | New York : Roaring Brook Press, 2017. |
   Audience: Ages 7–12. | "A Neal Porter Book." | Includes bibliographical
   references.

Identifiers: LCCN 2016025024 | ISBN 9781596439504 (hardcover)

Subjects: LCSH: Geology—Arizona—Grand Canyon—Juvenile literature. |
   Natural history—Arizona—Grand Canyon—Juvenile literature. | Grand
   Canyon (Ariz.) —Juvenile literature.

Classification: LCC F788 .C485 2017 | DDC 557.9132—dc23

LC record available at https://lccn.loc.gov/2016025024

Our books may be purchased in bulk for promotional, educational, or business use. Please
contact your local bookseller or the Macmillan Corporate and Premium Sales Department
at (800) 221-7945 ext. 5442 or by e-mail at MacmillanSpecialMarkets@macmillan.com.

First edition 2017

Printed in China by Toppan Leefung Printing Ltd., Dongguan City, Guangdong Province

1   3   5   7   9   10   8   6   4   2

Rivers carve canyons.

When they cut down into the earth, canyons grow deeper.

As weathering and erosion break apart their walls, canyons grow wider.

Over time, rivers wash all of the eroded material away.

These processes have been at work for millions of years,
relentlessly excavating the mighty gorge known as . . .

GRAND CANYON

JASON CHIN

A NEAL PORTER BOOK
ROARING BROOK PRESS
NEW YORK

Grand Canyon is one of the largest canyons in the world. It is 277 miles long, as much as 18 miles wide, and more than a mile deep, but it's much more than just a big hole in the ground.

It's home to an astonishing variety of plants and animals. The canyon is much hotter and drier at the bottom than at the top. Because of this, different groups of plants and animals, or ecological communities, are found at different elevations in the canyon. The hottest part of the canyon is at the very bottom, a thousand-foot-deep chasm called the Inner Gorge.

The Inner Gorge may be the hottest part of the canyon, but there are oases in this desert.

ECOLOGICAL COMMUNITIES IN GRAND CANYON

Elevations are approximate.

Boreal Forest
Elevation: Above 8,200 feet

Ponderosa Pine Forest
Elevation: 7,000 to 8,200 feet

Pinyon-Juniper Woodland
Elevation: 4,000 to 7,000 feet

Desert Scrub
Elevation: Below 4,000 feet

Riparian
Along rivers and streams at all elevations

Raccoon

Spotted sandpiper

Canyon tree frog

Lucy's warbler

Desert willow

Creeks bring life-giving water into the gorge, and a wide variety of species live along their banks, including frogs, dragonflies, mule deer, and the endangered southwestern willow flycatcher. Many of these creatures are permanent residents that rely on running water for survival, while others are visitors, drawn here by their thirst.

Mourning cloak

Red-spotted toad

Spotted skunk

Blue grosbeak

Cattails

Tree lizard

Beaver

Flame skimmer dragonfly

Cottonwood

Arizona bark scorpion

Eventually every creek in the canyon flows into the largest stream of all . . .

American ...er

Spotted bat

Netleaf hackberry

Southwestern willow flycatcher

Redbud

ROCK LAYERS IN GRAND CANYON

Dates are approximate.

Kaibab Formation: 270 million years old

Toroweap Formation: 273 million years old

Coconino Sandstone: 275 million years old

Hermit Formation: 280 million years old

Supai Group: 315 to 285 million years old

Surprise Canyon Formation:
320 million years old

Redwall Limestone:
340 million years old

Temple Butte Formation:
385 million years old

Muav Limestone:
505 million years old

Bright Angel Shale:
515 million years old

Tapeats Sandstone: 525 million years old

Inner Gorge

Grand Canyon Supergroup:
1,200 to around 740 million years old

Vishnu Basement Rocks:
1,840 to 1,680 million years old

Colorado River

. . . the Colorado River. The Colorado runs the entire length of Grand Canyon, continually washing sediment away and slowly deepening its channel. It's been cutting into the land for around 5 million years, slicing through layer after layer of rock. Today, it is cutting into the Vishnu Basement Rocks. These rocks are part of the continental basement— the bottommost layer of rock on the continent.

The basement rocks are the oldest in the canyon—as much as 1.84 *billion* years old. Many younger rock layers are stacked on top of them. If you hike out of the canyon you'll pass younger and younger layers as you climb, as if walking up through time.

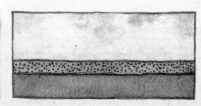

Starting more than a billion years ago, layers of sediment (such as sand and mud) piled up on top of the basement rocks, one after another.

Sediment Layers

Basement Rocks

Above the basement layer, you'll reach the Grand Canyon Supergroup. Here you may find ripple marks preserved in the stone. Clues like these tell us what this place was like when the rock formed. They are like windows . . .

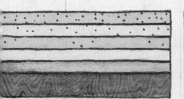

...er time, the layers of sediment turned into layers of solid rock (...ch as sandstone and mudstone).

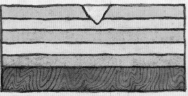

Rock Layers

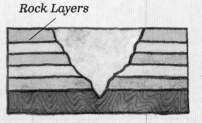

Much later, Grand Canyon was carved into these layers. The youngest layers are at the top and the oldest layers are at the bottom.

. . . to the past.

This is Grand Canyon, 1.2 billion years ago, when the only living things on Earth were microbes, such as algae and bacteria. Although they were too small to see, these primitive organisms filled the oceans, and were some of the earliest life-forms on the planet.

The mud from this tidal flat eventually transformed into a layer of solid rock and these ripple marks were preserved in the process. They are now part of the Grand Canyon Supergroup.

Spiny lizard

Antelope ground squirrel

Banana yucca

Rock pocket mouse

Desert tortoise

After climbing out of the Inner Gorge, you'll find yourself on a broad, sun-baked slope. The plants and animals here are well adapted for life with little water. Black-throated sparrows can go for long periods without taking a drink. Many creatures sleep during the heat of the day. Pocket mice forage at night and are preyed on by owls and rattlesnakes, who are adapted for hunting in the dark.

Canyon wren

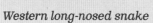
Western long-nosed snake

Black-throated sparrow

Collared lizard

Kangaroo rat

rsage

Ringtail

California barrel cactus

Black-tailed
jackrabbit

Chuckwalla

These animals are living on the rock layer called the Bright Angel Shale, which formed more than 200 million years after the Grand Canyon Supergroup. Trilobite fossils in the rocks tell us that this spot . . .

Mormon tea

Desert shrew

Blackbrush

Grand Canyon
rattlesnake

Grizzly bear cactus

. . . once lay beneath the sea.

This is Grand Canyon, 515 million years ago. By this time
in Earth's history many multicellular plants and animals had
evolved. Soft-bodied jellyfish floated above clam-like brachiopods
and tiny hyolithes, some of the first creatures on Earth with
shells. Trilobites, the first animals known to have had eyes,
roamed the sea floor. Around them, worm-like creatures
burrowed in the sediment—sediment that eventually
transformed into the Bright Angel Shale.

Towering over the Bright Angel Shale is a massive cliff called the Redwall Limestone. The Redwall has many inaccessible caves that provide nesting spots for one of the rarest birds in the world: the California condor.

The sea covered the Grand Canyon region many times in the past.

As the sea level rose, layers of sediment, composed of sand, mud, and shells, piled up.

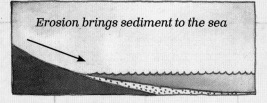

Erosion brings sediment to the sea

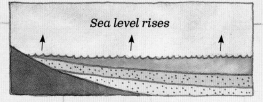

Sea level rises

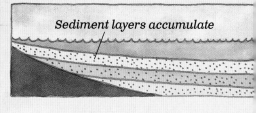

Sediment layers accumulate

With a 9-foot wingspan, and weighing as much as 23 pounds, the condor is the largest land bird in North America. Condors are vultures, and during the ice age they fed on the carcasses of mega-beasts like giant ground sloths. Since then, their population has declined due to changes in climate and human activity, and now they are close to extinction.

The sediment was compacted and cemented together over time and became sedimentary rock. Different types of sediment became different types of rock.

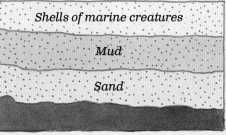

Shells of marine creatures

Mud

Sand

Limestone

Mudstone and Shale

Sandstone

Above the Redwall cliff is a slope of rust-red rock. The climate here is not as hot and dry as below, and pinyon pines and Utah junipers are common. Many creatures such as squirrels, chipmunks, and woodrats eat their seeds. These small rodents are preyed on by gopher snakes and coyotes.

Pinyon jay

Pinyon jays feast on pine nuts but they don't eat them all. They bury some and let them grow. The trees feed the jays and the jays plant new trees. Together they help sustain the pinyon-juniper ecosystem.

Desert cottontail

Pereg...
fa...

Gray fox

Utah juniper

Raven

Cliff chipmunk

Cliffrose

At the top of the slope is the rock layer called the Hermit Formation. Fossils in the Hermit tell us that long ago, this spot was home to . . .

Northern pygmy owl

Pinyon mouse

Coyote

Broom snakeweed

Townsend's solitaire

. . . huge dragonflies with 8-inch wingspans.

This is Grand Canyon 280 million years ago. By this time, life was flourishing on land and trees, ferns, fish, amphibians, and reptiles had evolved. The sea had retreated from the region and rivers flowed across the landscape. Seed ferns and conifers grew along their banks, and amphibians left their tracks in the mud—mud that eventually transformed into the Hermit Formation.

Above the red slopes of the Hermit are pale 350-foot cliffs. Bighorn sheep easily navigate their narrow ledges with specially adapted hooves. In the fall mating season, males compete for dominance by smashing into each other with their battering ram horns.

As Grand Canyon's rock layers were deposited, the remains of plants and animals were buried, and some became fossils.

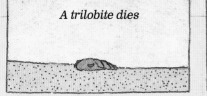

A trilobite dies

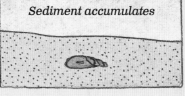

Sediment accumulates

Shell becomes fossil as sediment becomes rock

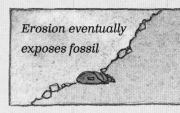

Erosion eventually exposes fossil

These cliffs have been carved from the Coconino Sandstone.
Fossil footprints in the rock tell us that on this spot 275
million years ago . . .

Fossils are the remains or traces of
ancient life that have been preserved
in rock. Most fossils are found in
sedimentary rock.

Fossil footprints and worm burrows
are called trace fossils.

Fossil skeletons and shells
are called body fossils.

. . . an early reptile walked across huge, windswept dunes.

With little water, life here would have been difficult, but the desert wasn't entirely barren. Among the other species that called it home were scorpions, millipedes, and spiders. As the desert wind whipped across the landscape, sand piled up in thin layers. Today those layers are preserved in the Coconino Sandstone as thin, angled surfaces called cross-beds.

As you approach the rim of the canyon, the climate becomes cooler and more moist. Vegetation on the sloping Toroweap Formation is more dense than below. Before exiting the canyon, however, there is one more layer to scale: the Kaibab Formation.

When rocks break apart, it's called weathering. When the broken pieces are carried away, it's called erosion. Ice and growing plants break up rocks in Grand Canyon and most of the sediment is removed from the canyon by water.

The Kaibab's limestone cliffs are full of marine fossils that tell us about life here 270 million years ago . . .

and Canyon's walls have both cliffs and pes because different layers erode in fferent ways. Sandstone and limestone tend break off in blocks leaving cliffs. Shale and udstone tend to crumble and form slopes. en shale erodes beneath limestone or ndstone, and the cliff wall gives way.

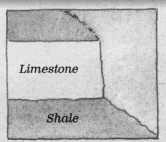

Limestone

Shale

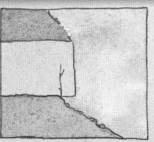

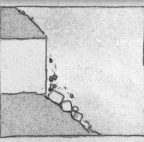

. . . when the ocean again covered the land.

Fossils in the Kaibab Formation tell of a complex ecosystem.
The sea floor was home to sea lilies and bryozoans, sponges and
coral. Trilobites and brachiopods lived alongside them, while
nautiloids and as many as forty species of shark patrolled the
water above them. Many of these creatures, such as coral
and brachiopods, had hard shells. When they died, their shells
piled up on the sea floor and eventually transformed into the
limestone of the Kaibab Formation.

Goshawk

Elk

Uinta chipmunk

American kestrel

Ponderosa pine

If you ascend from the Colorado River to the South Rim of Grand Canyon you will have climbed nearly 5,000 feet and passed through three distinct habitats. Above the rim, you'll find one more.

Evening grosbeak

Abert's squirrel

Kaibab squirrel

Wild turkey

Str
sku

Western bluebird

Mountain lion

Porcupine

Hairy woodpecker

Gambel oak

The Ponderosa pine forest is home to tassel-eared squirrels, deer, and elk. Bobcats, coyotes, and hawks hunt here, as well as the top predators in the canyon: mountain lions.

eller's jay

Mountain mahogany

Bobcat

Great horned owl

Turkey vulture

. . . the grandest canyon on Earth.

Because of its great size and depth, Grand Canyon has a wide range of climates and habitats, and species that call the canyon home today survive on ancient rocks—rocks that tell us about life here long before there was a canyon.

It's taken millions of years of weathering and erosion to expose these rocks and shape this breathtaking landscape, and these processes continue to this day, relentlessly excavating . . .

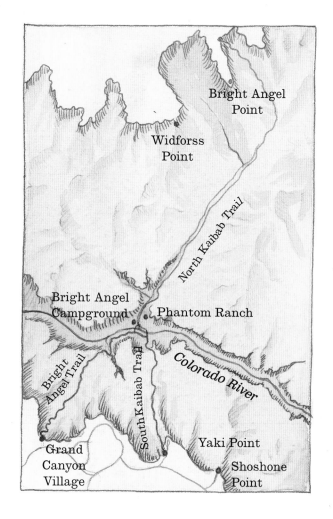

THE GRANDEST CANYON

This book depicts a journey across Grand Canyon from the North to the South Rim. The mountain lion roughly follows the North Kaibab Trail into the canyon. The girl and her father begin near Phantom Ranch and take the South Kaibab Trail up to the South Rim. On their combined journeys, they witness a wide range of habitats and geologic features. Yet, despite travelling roughly 20 miles, descending a vertical mile down and up again, they've only seen a fraction of Grand Canyon. The canyon is simply too big for any one person to see it all, even in a lifetime of study. Its size, however, is just part of what makes Grand Canyon grand. The canyon is mind-bogglingly old, has a rich cultural history, a fascinating ecology, and its geologic significance is second to none. It is the combination of these impressive elements that make it the grandest canyon on Earth.

area shown at left

HUMAN HISTORY

Humans have been visiting and living in the canyon for at least 12,000 years. The earliest people to come to the Grand Canyon region hunted big game with stone-tipped spears and lived a nomadic life. Later, several different cultures settled in and around the canyon, including the Ancestral Puebloans, farmers and skilled potters who lived in multi-room buildings called pueblos. Today's Hopi and Zuni peoples trace their heritage to the Ancestral Puebloans. It wasn't until Hopi guides led Spanish explorers to the South Rim in 1540 that the first Europeans saw Grand Canyon.

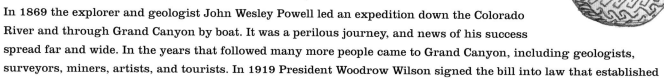

In 1869 the explorer and geologist John Wesley Powell led an expedition down the Colorado River and through Grand Canyon by boat. It was a perilous journey, and news of his success spread far and wide. In the years that followed many more people came to Grand Canyon, including geologists, surveyors, miners, artists, and tourists. In 1919 President Woodrow Wilson signed the bill into law that established Grand Canyon National Park, and today more than four million people visit the park each year. The park covers more than one million acres of land and most of the canyon lies inside the park boundary, while parts of it are within the borders of the Hualapai, Havasupai, and Navajo Indian reservations. The canyon remains a place of cultural and spiritual importance for many Native American tribes, including the Hopi, Navajo, Zuni, Paiute, Apache, Hualapai, and Havasupai.

GRAND CANYON ECOLOGY

Grand Canyon is home to thousands of species, including 373 birds, 92 mammals, 1,750 plants, and more than 8,000 invertebrates. Twenty-nine species are endemic to the canyon, meaning they don't live anywhere else on Earth. This wide variety of life is due to the canyon's topography, or physical structure. Its rugged landscape and in particular its great depth have a significant effect on climate throughout the canyon. The lower the elevation, the hotter and drier the canyon becomes. Because of the variation in climate, specific groups of plants and animals called ecological communities live at different elevations—and these communities can be *very* different. Hiking into the canyon has been compared to walking from the forests of Canada to the deserts of Mexico in a matter of hours!

Prominent Ecological Communities in Grand Canyon

Elevations are approximate. Communities usually transition gradually from one to the next and may be found outside the listed range.

Boreal Forest
Above 8,200 feet
Boreal, or northern, forests of spruce and fir grow on the canyon's North Rim only, because the North Rim is about 1,000 feet higher than the South Rim.

Ponderosa Pine Forest
7,000 to 8,200 feet
Ponderosa pine forests are found on both rims and in some places below the rim of the canyon.

Pinyon-Juniper Woodland
4,000 to 7,000 feet
Pinyon pines and Utah junipers are drought tolerant trees and anchor this desert woodland community.

Desert Scrub
Below 4,000 feet
Species from the three deserts that border the canyon are found in Grand Canyon: the Great Basin Desert to the north, the Mojave to the west, and the Sonoran to the south.

Riparian
Along rivers and streams at all elevations
Riparian communities surround and depend on flowing water, such as rivers and streams. They have the greatest wildlife diversity of all habitats in the canyon.

GRAND CANYON GEOLOGY

Grand Canyon has one of the most remarkable sequences of rock layers found anywhere in the world. The age of its rocks spans more than 1.5 billion years (about a third of the age of Earth) and geologists have learned a lot about the deep history of the region from studying these rocks. Each rock layer formed at a different time and in a different environment, and the rocks tell us about these environments. Like detectives, geologists look for clues in the rocks and use them to piece together a picture of the past. Common clues that geologists study are fossils, sedimentary structures, and the type of rock.

Sedimentary Rock

Most of Grand Canyon's layers are made of sedimentary rock. Sedimentary rock forms when loose sediment is transported, deposited, and then compacted and cemented into solid rock over time. These sedimentary rocks help geologists decipher what the environment was like when the sediment was being deposited. For example, limestone is often made up of the shells of marine creatures, so a limestone layer suggests an ocean environment. Shale, which comes from mud, may suggest a mudflat or river bank, and sandstone, which comes from sand, suggests a desert, a river, or a sandy beach.

Rock Structures

Sediment often retains its structure as it turns to stone, telling us what the surface of the land looked like in the distant past. Raindrop impressions in mudstone record the moment when rain fell on the muddy earth, while ripple marks tell of ancient mudflats or riverbeds.

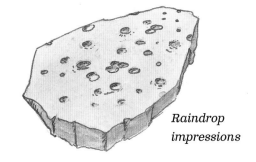

Raindrop impressions

Fossils

Almost every layer in Grand Canyon has fossils. The fossils give us a glimpse of ecosystems that existed when the layers formed. Sea shells tell us about marine ecosystems, while footprints tell us about terrestrial (on land) environments.

Since the layers in Grand Canyon are in sequence from oldest to youngest, they also give us a picture of how life in the region changed over time. The oldest fossils are in the Grand Canyon Supergroup rocks, which date from the Precambrian—the period in Earth's history when life first appeared. The fossils in these rocks include stromatolites (structures made by bacteria) and microfossils such as amoeba.

Moving up the canyon to younger rocks (and forward in time), more complex species start to appear. Trilobites and the burrows of worm-like organisms appear in the layers above the Supergroup. Terrestrial species, including reptile tracks, seed ferns, and trees, appear in the Hermit Formation and the Coconino Sandstone nearer to the top of the canyon.

Reptile tracks

Seed fern

Trilobite

Amoeba

HOW CANYONS ARE CARVED

Canyons are carved by rivers, but not all rivers carve canyons. To cut a canyon, a river must flow across high terrain and carry sediment in its water. The elevated land gives the river something to carve into, and the higher the elevation, the deeper the canyon can be. The actual carving is done not by river water, but by sediment in the water. As sand, gravel, and, most importantly, boulders, roll downstream and strike the river bottom, they chip away at the bedrock and deepen the canyon. The more sediment there is, and the larger the rocks, the greater the river's ability to deepen its channel. Canyons grow wider as their walls erode and send debris tumbling into their rivers. This added sediment increases the river's cutting ability as it is washed downstream and eventually removed from the canyon.

Rivers deepen canyons when sediment chips away at the bedrock.

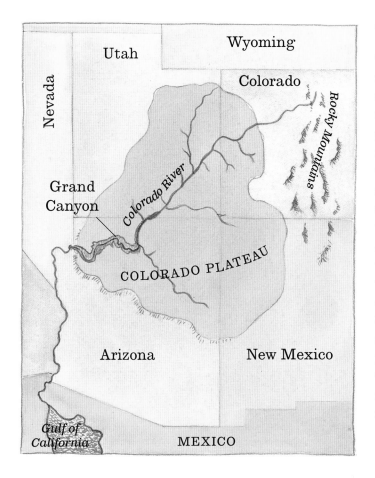

THE COLORADO RIVER

The Colorado River flows from the Rocky Mountains to the Gulf of California and on the way it crosses a broad area of elevated land called the Colorado Plateau. Grand Canyon has been cut into the southwestern edge of the plateau. A lot of sediment washes into the Colorado River from the arid landscape, turning its water rust red, which is how the river got its name—*Rio Colorado* means "red river" in Spanish. In the spring, melting snow from the Rockies floods the river, and with all of that extra water, comes more and larger-sized sediment. Although flooding in the canyon is now controlled by the Glen Canyon Dam upstream, large floods did rage through Grand Canyon in the past (the dam also traps sediment behind it, so the river is no longer muddy in Grand Canyon). It's thought that the canyon was carved primarily during these floods, and that during prehistoric times mega-floods carried car-sized boulders through the canyon! The river's location on the Colorado Plateau, the availability of sediment, and its annual floods, all contributed to the carving of Grand Canyon.

GRAND MYSTERY

Although the processes that carve canyons are understood, nobody knows exactly how Grand Canyon was carved. In fact, nobody even knows how old Grand Canyon is! Geologists agree that the Colorado River has been running on its present course for 6 to 5 million years, and for a long time it was thought that the canyon is as old as the river. Recent evidence suggests, however, that the canyon may be much older than the modern Colorado River and that other rivers started carving the canyon before the Colorado. Different geologists have different ideas about the specific details and timeline of the canyon's formation. They actively debate them and are working to uncover new evidence that will support or disprove their ideas. We may never know the full story, but stay tuned—more evidence is bound to turn up and shed new light on the carving of Grand Canyon.

THE STORY IN THE ROCKS

The layers of rock exposed in the walls of Grand Canyon are stacked in sequence from oldest to youngest. Each layer tells us what the region was like when that layer was deposited, and together they tell us how the region changed over time. Geologists can "read" the layers like pages in a book, and after years of careful study, they've pieced together the story in the rocks. The story starts at the bottom, with the formation of the basement rocks:

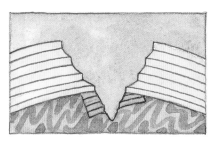

5. Grand Canyon Is Carved
At some point after the uplift of the Colorado Plateau began, Grand Canyon began to be carved. After at least 5 million years of excavation, the canyon now reaches all the way down to the basement rocks.

4. The Colorado Plateau Rises
Between 70 and 40 million years ago, tectonic forces lifted up the basement rocks and all the layers on top of them. Today, the uplifted land is known as the Colorado Plateau.

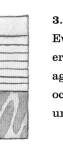

3. Horizontal Layers Deposited
Eventually most of the Supergroup rocks eroded away. Then, starting 525 million years ago, many rock layers were deposited as the ocean rose and fell, alternately covering and uncovering the land.

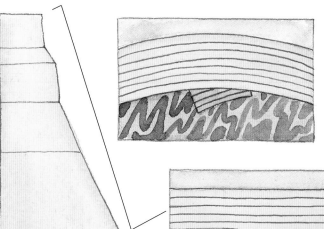

2. The Supergroup Forms and Tilts
Starting about 1,250 million years ago, the rock layers of the Grand Canyon Supergroup piled up on top of the basement rocks. Then faulting caused the land to break and tilt. This is why the Grand Canyon Supergroup layers are at an angle.

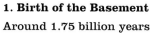

1. Birth of the Basement
Around 1.75 billion years ago, forces deep within the Earth caused an island chain to crash into ancient North America. Heat and pressure from the collision created the basement rocks.

A NOTE FROM THE AUTHOR

 As I was researching this book, I tried to imagine how the region changed over time and was "bit by the geology bug" (as my advisor, Wayne Ranney, put it). It fascinates me that I can look at a rock and with a basic understanding of geology, know something of its past. Now, when I look at rocks, I can't help trying to imagine their history, where they came from, and the story of how they formed. This book is my tribute to the canyon and also to the power of the imagination. After all, it's imagination that makes both science and art possible. I hope that this book captures my readers' imaginations, just as Grand Canyon has captured mine.

A Note on the Illustrations

With a few exceptions, my characters travel to places that I went when I visited Grand Canyon. Each illustration in this book depicts a location along specific trails and if you visit the canyon you may be able to find the very spots that I included. There are two discrepancies, however, that you may notice. The first is that the Shoshone Point Trail (where the characters see the Ponderosa pine forest) is not immediately accessible from the top of the South Kaibab Trail. To get from one to the other requires a short car ride. To maintain continuity in the story, I left my characters' car out of the book.

The second is with the fossils that the girl finds on her hike. They are based on actual fossils that have been found in Grand Canyon, but the real fossils aren't by the side of the trail where she finds them. Some are in collections, others are off the trail or on other trails. To make the story work I put them where she could easily see them. If you go to Grand Canyon, you may not find fossils where they appear in the book, but there are many fossils to see on trails, along the rim, and in exhibits in Grand Canyon Village. If you do happen to find a fossil, please leave it where you found it so that others might discover it and so scientists may study it. Collecting fossils or other natural objects inside Grand Canyon National Park is not allowed.

Finally, the reader should know that the illustrations of past environments in this book are depictions of what the environments *might* have looked like. To create them, I worked with Christa Sadler and David Elliott to make each scene as accurate as possible. In each picture I primarily included species that actually appear as fossils in or near Grand Canyon, with the exception of a few soft-bodied species such as algae and jellies that were likely present, but rarely fossilize.

For many of the species, there was very little fossil evidence to inform my illustrations. For example, the early reptiles in the Coconino are only known from their tracks. As we don't have any evidence of what their bodies looked like, I placed the creature in silhouette. The sharks in the Kaibab are only known from their teeth, but body fossils of related sharks have been found (not in Grand Canyon) so I based my illustrations on those fossils. There are many things, however, that I had to invent entirely, such as atmosphere, light, and color. The images are based on research, but brought to life with my imagination.

ACKNOWLEDGMENTS

I had help with my research from four experts whose knowledge of Grand Canyon far exceeds mine. I'd like to thank each of them for their patience, guidance, and support. Without their help this book would not have been possible.

Wayne Ranney
Grand Canyon geologist and author

Stewart Aitchison
Naturalist and author

Christa Sadler
Geologist, educator, guide, and author

Dr. David K. Elliott
Paleontologist in the Geology Program at Northern Arizona University

Special thanks to Lili Epstein, Cyrus Roxas, and Kate Hansen-Roxas

SELECTED SOURCES

Books

Abbott, Lon, and Terri Cook. *Hiking the Grand Canyon's Geology*. Seattle: The Mountaineers Books, 2004.

Beus, Stanley S., and Michael Morales, Eds. *Grand Canyon Geology,* Second Edition. New York: Oxford University Press, 2003.

Blakey, Ron, and Wayne Ranney. *Ancient Landscapes of the Colorado Plateau*. Grand Canyon: Grand Canyon Association, 2008.

Brown, Bryan T., Steve W. Carothers, and R. Roy Johnson. *Grand Canyon Birds*. Tuscon: The University of Arizona Press, 1986.

Coder, Chistopher M. *An Introduction to Grand Canyon Prehistory*. Grand Canyon: Grand Canyon Association, 2000.

DK Publishing. *Prehistoric Life: The Definitive Visual History of Life on Earth*. New York: Dorling Kindersley, 2009.

Foster, John. *Cambrian Ocean World: Ancient Sea Life of North America*. Bloomington: Indiana University Press, 2014.

Hoffmeister, Donald F. *Mammals of Grand Canyon*. Chicago: University of Illinois Press, 1971.

Houk, Rose. *An Introduction to Grand Canyon Ecology*. Grand Canyon: Grand Canyon Association, 1996.

Johnson, Kirk R., and Richard K. Stucky. *Prehistoric Journey: A History of Life on Earth*. Golden, CO: Fulcrum Publishing, 2006.

Knoll, Andrew H. *Life on a Young Planet: The First Three Billion Years of Evolution on Earth*. Princeton: Princeton University Press, 2003.

Lamb, Susan. *Grand Canyon Wildlife: Rim to River*. Grand Canyon: Grand Canyon Association, 2013.

Mathez, Edmond A., and James D. Webster. *The Earth Machine: The Science of a Dynamic Planet*. New York: Columbia University Press, 2007.

Price, L. Greer. *An Introduction to Grand Canyon Geology*. Grand Canyon: The Grand Canyon Association, 1999.

Ranney, Wayne. *Carving Grand Canyon: Evidence, Theories and Mystery,* Second Edition. Grand Canyon: Grand Canyon Association, 2012.

Sadler, Christa. *Life in Stone: Fossils of the Colorado Plateau*. Grand Canyon: Grand Canyon Association, 2005.

Thayer, Dave. *An Introduction to Grand Canyon Fossils*. Grand Canyon: The Grand Canyon Association, 2009.

White, David. *Flora of the Hermit Shale, Grand Canyon, Arizona*. Washington: Carnegie Institution of Washington, 1929.

Whitney, Stephen R. *A Field Guide to the Grand Canyon,* Second Edition. Seattle: The Mountaineers Books, 1996.

Websites

"Geologic Glossary," *USGS Geology in the Parks*, USGS
geomaps.wr.usgs.gov/parks/misc/glossarya.html

"Lexicon of Colorado Plateau Stratigraphy," *Geology of the National Parks*, USGS
3dparks.wr.usgs.gov/coloradoplateau/lexicon/

"Park Profile 2014," *Grand Canyon National Park* (National Park Service)
nps.gov/grca/learn/management/upload/2014-grca-park-profile.pdf

"Park Statistics," *Grand Canyon National Park* (National Park Service)
nps.gov/grca/learn/management/statistics.htm

Papers

Dealer, C. M., Porter S. M., and Timmons, J. M., "The Neo-poterozoic Earth Sytem Revealed from the Chuar Group of Grand Canyon." *Grand Canyon Geology, Two Billion Years of Earth's History*: The Geological Society of America Special Paper 489, 2012.

Hodnett, J-P., Elliot, D. K. and Olson, T. J., "A New Basal Hybodont (Chondrichthyes, Hybodontiformes) from the Middle Permian (Roadian) Kaibab Formation, of Northern Arizona." *The Carboniferous-Permian Transition*: New Mexico Museum of Natural History and Science Bulletin 60, 2013.

Hollingsworth, J. S., Sundberg, F. A., and Foster, J. R., (editors), *Cambian Stratigraphy and Paleontology of Northern Arizona and Southern Nevada*: Museum of Northern Arizona Bulletin 67, 2011.

FOR FURTHER READING

Aliki. *Fossils Tell of Long Ago*. New York: HarperCollins, 1990.

Buchheit, Mike. *Going to Grand Canyon National Park*. Helena, MO: Farcountry Press, 2012.

Garton Scanlon, Liz, illustrated by Ashley Wolff. *In the Canyon*. New York: Beach Lane Books, 2015.

Minor, Wendell. *Grand Canyon: Exploring a Natural Wonder*. New York: Scholastic, 1998.

O'Connor, Jim, illustrated by Daniel Colón. *Where Is the Grand Canyon?* New York: Grosset and Dunlap, 2015.

Viera, Linda, illustrated by Christopher Canyon. *Grand Canyon: A Trail Through Time*. New York: Walker Children's, 2000.

Waldman, Stuart, illustrated by Gregory Manchess. *The Last River: John Wesley Powell and the Colorado River*. New York: Mikaya Press, 2015.

GRAND CANYON
GENERALIZED CROSS SECTION

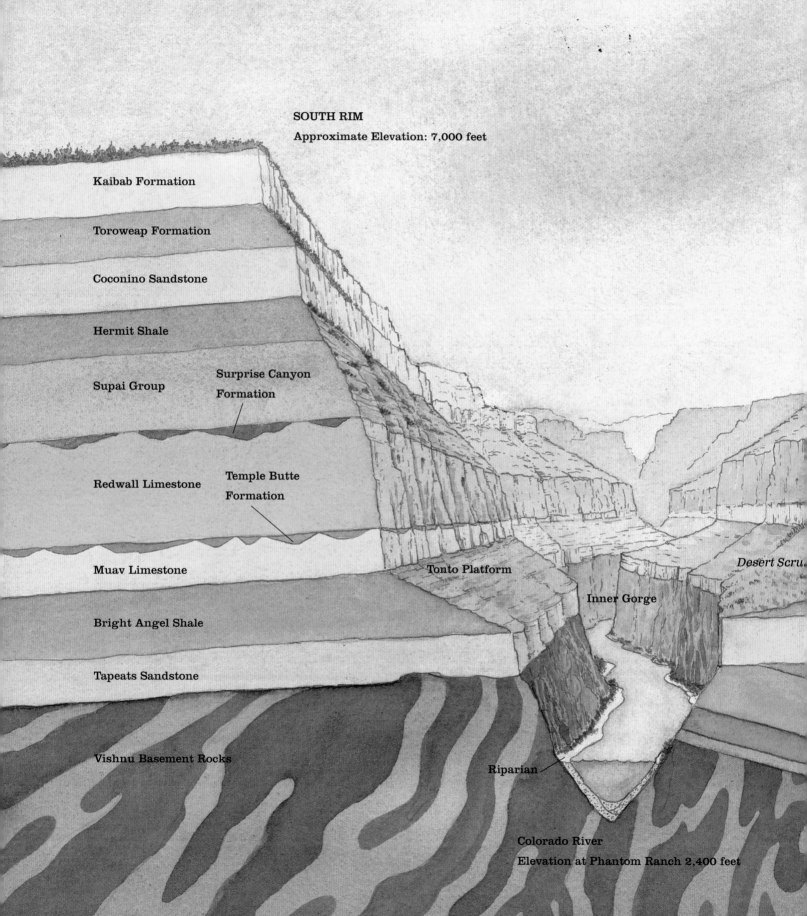

SOUTH RIM
Approximate Elevation: 7,000 feet

Kaibab Formation

Toroweap Formation

Coconino Sandstone

Hermit Shale

Supai Group

Surprise Canyon
Formation

Redwall Limestone

Temple Butte
Formation

Muav Limestone

Tonto Platform

Desert Scru.

Inner Gorge

Bright Angel Shale

Tapeats Sandstone

Vishnu Basement Rocks

Riparian

Colorado River

Elevation at Phantom Ranch 2,400 feet